I0755917

FINISHING LINE PRESS
www.finishinglinepress.com

All That Blue

poems by

Allison Field Bell

Finishing Line Press
Georgetown, Kentucky

All That Blue

ISBN 979-8-89990-396-0 First Edition

Thanks to the following journals for publishing my work:

Ruminate: "Girl in My Youth"
Nimrod International Journal: "What Could Belong to Us" and "Paros"
Palette Poetry: "Sonoran Desert"
Superstition Review: "Ketura" and "Threshold"
The Shore: "Windows Open to the Night"
Sugar House Review: "Garden"
The Greensboro Review: "Anatomy Lesson"
RHINO Poetry: "Coalesce"
Shō Poetry Journal: "Barcelona"
South Dakota Review: "Grandmother Ethel"
The South Carolina Review: "You Burn Me"
THRUSH Poetry Journal: "Four Walls Become a Woman"
Lunch Ticket: "You have to run open mouthed"
Cream City Review: "The Girls"
Poetry Online: "She Climbs In"
Passages North: "Teacup Rose" and "Horse Girl"
Smartish Pace: "Last Week"
The Pinch: "O'Keeffe Country"
Pigeon Pages: "Against Her"
The Paddock Review: "How to Write a Poem Without Woman or Body" and "Skeleton"

A selection of poems also appears in WITHOUT WOMAN OR BODY (Finishing Line Press Summer 2025)

Publisher: Leah Huete de Maines
Editor: Christen Kincaid
Cover Art and Design: Sarah Williams
Author Photo: Jasmine Khaliq

Order online: www.finishinglinepress.com
also available on amazon.com

Author inquiries and mail orders:
Finishing Line Press
PO Box 1626
Georgetown, Kentucky 40324
USA

Contents

III

IV

For all my loves who keep believing in the poetry part of my brain—
you know who you are

Garden

I haven't been honest with myself. The peony in my front
yard had just one bloom last year. Fleeting, fuchsia.

I watched it unfurl one petal at a time, breaking through the bud.
Couldn't leave the house for fear of it happening without me.

Stared through the window in pajamas. Days lost to waiting.
My doctor wants to increase my medication—he suggests we double it,

my brain needs more than it already has. I think about the quartet of tulips in the
backyard—every winter I fear they must have died down there

but every spring they shoot through the ground in a great miracle—
green stalks and deep wine-red blossoms. I tell my doctor this. A metaphor.

Really, I wonder how long any of us can last. Winters changing: rain in
February in Utah. The whole of the Salt Lake Valley under threat.

Beneath the lake's liquid skin: poison. The last medication I tried flooded my heart
in a ruthless double-beat. I couldn't do anything right:

drink coffee, pour wine. I yelled at my doctor on the phone. He agreed
that it was wrong. Told me I shouldn't be drinking. Too much

for my liver to hold. There's also a bed of irises that bloom
later than the rest: early summer and their pale pink flesh opens

to the mountain heat. Doctor doesn't understand why I'm talking
about bulbs, about flowers. Why I can't just say I want to get better.

I tell him, I wish I could just live outside. Plant me in the yard, let me
disappear in winter and return come spring. Let me be brief and full of light.

I

Horse Girl

As a child, I raised guppies. Bright scaled creatures that fluttered through freshwater. They multiplied overnight, filling the tank with color. I netted the babies to separate them, so they wouldn't be consumed. When they were big enough, I sold them for a few dollars to a local pet store. I was saving to buy a horse. A useless enterprise. I wanted something to carry me across the earth. All that muscle. Large liquid eyes. The smell of alfalfa and hay. Instead, I had cages. Tanks. Green anoles, hermit crabs, a teddy bear hamster, the guppies. My room a menagerie of what I could afford. The horse I dreamed up was a proud unbroken mare. And I wouldn't be the one to break her—no one would—but she would only respond to me. My touch. My voice. A way of being something other than myself. Maybe every little girl's fantasy. I didn't know how to be otherwise. Makeup, shaved legs, boys. But I wasn't a horse girl either. I was guppy girl. I saved the boldest most beautiful males for breeding. Their tails a spectacle. Watching them shimmer. Running the numbers in my head. Heart in a gallop.

Skeleton

I have tried to paint the bones and the blue —Georgia O'Keeffe

In my backyard, field
of grass tall as a toddler.
Knees in dirt, tunneling
through warm green. I buried
a lizard here—a green anole—
believing its body would become
bones. Skeletal. Tiny reptilian
skull, every limb thinner than
a toothpick. I lost track of it—
so many years ago. Sink my
hands into earth, find nothing.
Instead, ladybugs cling to
slender stems, beings like tiny
buttons, their crisp exterior:
one whole round red bone.
I cannot help myself: I want
to crush them. The familiar
pop, pulp on my skin. But I am
no longer that child, just a woman
hoping for lizard bones,
standing up against sheer blue
a stain of wings, circling, circling.

Especially Heinous

As a teenager, I looked for monsters. Serial killers, cult leaders, kidnappers, and the kind of man who catcalls a child on a country road. I watched hours and hours of *Law and Order.* Haunted by images of bodies. Mostly women. Mostly *SVU*. And what is a monster if not a body? The way it moves and rests. Its sick flesh features: face, torso, limbs. And the heart: that thick muscled center. I always want to see what they don't want to show me. The mangled legs of a victim. I want to see the blood. At eight, I cheated on my first spelling test. I grew older: called a girl fat, betrayed my brother, drove into one car, backed into another. Seventeen: slept with my friend's boyfriend. Eighteen: fucked any man who looked at me or sometimes he didn't look. Wasn't I a wreck? Wasn't I a monster? A kind of virus. Living off the living.

The Girls

We want / sex. Girls / budding / into bodies
breasts and mascara / and breasts / we
show to / boys: still just unrealized
/ hormones / walking / mesmerized
by underwear / catalogs. / And then
a party / chests against / windows.
They cannot / look at a daughter / the same
something / beyond / a departure.
Little girl / in horse dress no longer / picking
pansies from the / garden / floating them in
plastic cups / tears over
scraped knee / stubbed toe / rose thorn
against / tender fingertip. / How /
can they look at us? How / should they
look / at us? Who /should be
allowed / to love us?

Road Trip

Sloppy joes in Winnemucca. Then the Great Salt Lake. Hot pools of Idaho. Our first moose in the Grand Tetons, our first bison in Yellowstone. Snow and a grizzly by the road. Old Faithful and her noxious spray. Speed across the badlands, watching prairie dogs scurry through dust. Photograph the men carved in granite, the corn palace of Iowa. Crush mosquitos in Minnesota, chase fireflies in Wisconsin. Father drives. My brother and I play poker for pennies. Five-card draw. Mother stares down a map, reads us stories of bear attacks. Outside the RV is thunder is lightning is blue sky is cloud is dark velvet blanket of stars. I am still so young. Before my mind changes. And in another life, it doesn't. I just drift side-to-side. One coast to the other. West to east. Pole-to-pole. A seesaw. I can't stay a child forever. We end in Massachusetts. End on a beach with a lighthouse. Horseshoe crabs, minnow nets. A millpond, a sea.

What Could Belong to Us

Stubborn little girls in a creek bed,
freshwater up to our knees,
looking for what we cannot name,
something we can own all of,
or maybe just: berries to eat,
tadpoles with legs, a tree root
to hold onto. In two decades, two
of us will have girl children
of our own. (Not me, not me.)
Two of us will wander room to
room in our own homes, aching
with milk. We will be so full
of love for our husbands.
(Not me, not me.) Rubber boots
so full of creek water, stubborn,
we trudge through the clear
gushing center: three girls
in a creek. Drain pipe under
the road, large enough to contain
us at this age, and when we lean
in to examine what must be the soft
dark moss of its belly, we see
spiders, millions of thin legs
moving. Our own legs moving
us away: voices echo, one scream
after another, another after another.
(Not me, not me.) Because here
I am still, riveted by them:
water stirring to my thighs,
a deep chill spreading.

Beneath the Roots

My mother says I've seen the world,
She says, *Look at all the places you've been.*

She says, *And all the homes you've made.*
In Salt Lake City, I'm digging a hole in my backyard.

I don't know what it's for but I know it will be
bigger. As a child, I believed I could dig

myself to another country, another world.
Small fingers clawing through earth.

Every evening, my mother scrubbed my nails
clean. Laughing one day, cursing another.

Her moods as mercurial as the weather. Full of heat
and then rain and then cold California night.

This hole in my backyard started out about grass. Dig down
beneath the roots. Grass in a high desert. Grass in a drought.

The hole is to my waist. Jump in every morning and remove
shovelfuls before work. Cool damp dirt at my sides. Imagine

being buried in it. Worms curling through my toes,
the unbearable pressure. My mother says it's wonderful

that I've traveled, that I am so adventurous. To live
in Indiana / New Mexico / Arizona / Utah. To live

in Ecuador / Israel / Greece / England. To follow my impulse.
She doesn't know how difficult it is to leave the house.

Check the stove, the door, the cat. Check and recheck
and recheck. I cannot see beyond the digging. The hole

looks like a trap like a home like a portal. Soon, I will
not be able to crawl my way out. Suspended below

the edges of the surface. Fantasize an airplane,
a train, a car. Something with motion and the in-between,

not quite home but not somewhere else. Here, I will
let go. Cat meowing, doors wide open, stove burners alight.

What it means to leave a place and to arrive. Hide out
until the sun rises in another time zone. Until I feel the damp

dew of morning. Don't know where I am anymore,
bare feet chilled and covered in the dirt that made me.

Girl In My Youth

Before her, I liked them. Their volume, their strength. Girl in my youth pulled at her own muscle there, telling me too much body for one body. And: running makes us ugly. Legs manly. Carved calves, thick thighs, soccer shin guard tan, slope down to the ankles, muscles I could flex. Defined and sturdy. She stood in front of the mirror: pinching, angling, sighing. Before her, I didn't want my body smaller. Before her, I didn't know I wanted to be like her. Her body, her legs. Her way of looking, hungry for some other body. Before her, I didn't know I wanted her. And after her too. For years, I didn't know how to want a body like mine. A girl can see another girl in the mirror, can fail to see the woman at her side.

Opossum Carcass

I am afraid
of no one:
death wish
all my own.
Light crawls
over field
and vineyard.

Arm stretched
over the yellow
line: one hand,
pink fingers curled
into a loose fist.

Cadillac

In one memory, he's driving a lemon-colored Cadillac down a narrow one-lane forest road. I have a migraine. Can't keep my eyes open—dappled light through the trees unbearable. He tells me about a car accident, painkillers, or maybe cocaine. Something to worry about later. The Cadillac is a boat, heavy and loud. Normally, I like the windows open, wind in my face, music vibrating the doors. The leather seats are sandy and worn. In California, I am always bringing sand with me. Sand caked to my shins. Sand in my scalp, in my purse. Ocean only a drive away. This is where we have been: the Pacific. I want the cold salt waves on my forehead. Numbing. I can't look at him. He talks in murmurs—a strain to listen to. Something about his friend. About a broken arm. A hospital. I don't know why I bother. But I like the bench seat in the front—I can lay my head in his lap. Feel the muscles of his legs shifting. Feel the heaving of the car's motor. Light through the trees on my eyelids, each flickering speck a point of pain. Road potholed and full of ache. And his voice: a lullaby now. Cadillac moving us forward, the solid shape of it carrying us.

Making Myself Quit

We painted our lips scarlet and stole
our mothers' heels, pointed leather pumps
stuffed with socks, shuffling over every surface.

We smoked fake cigarettes—paper that expelled
powder. Grew obsessed, holding them between
fingers, like the adult I didn't even want

to be. Smuggled them upstairs in the garage,
smoking by the open window. The girl who,
years later, in college, would smoke her first

real cigarette on a rooftop, stars swept
across the sky, a crisp cold night. To impress
a Devon or David or maybe Zach, inhaled

one toxic breath after another, lungs burning,
face burning. There on the rooftop, the fake
cigarettes: the addiction, making myself quit,

hiding two sticks of paper and powder deep
in the trash can. On the rooftop,
Devon or David or Zach leaned in

to kiss me, and we did. Mouths like two ash trays
colliding. I felt alone, the way I did after
shaving my legs that first time, skin

smooth and blank. Sat on the edge
of the tub and wept, not for what was
missing, but wondering where I would end up next.

II

Ketura

I.
Dusk
copper cloaked, acacia
silhouettes. I'm
in my freebox skirt,
cut-sleeve t-shirt. Glass
of arak, mint leaf suspended
above ice. here, now,
the worst worry is animal.
Snake, spider, solifuge.
I wander among rocks,
sipping, watching my
skin go gold.

II.
Just last night,
I had a man here, out
in the desert, at the date palm
roofed mud hut, built
by children. He dragged
a mattress out to
fuck me. Now, in the dust,
alone, I practice saying
no. No thank you, I say
to the warm evening air.
I kick a rock, watch it
stir up a tiny cloud.

III.
Wasn't even him
I wanted. His girlfriend:
long black hair, laughter
contagious. I didn't know
how to say that either. How
to think it. She will not
forgive me. Later, she will call
me *American slut.* *American*
whore. *Bitch.* Later

still, she will marry him,
have his two children.

IV.

Right now,   alone,   I
                    can hear   the military in
          their adjacent desert.   Distant
     crack of weapons.   This place:
     riddled with war.
                    Stars flicker
to life.   Soon the sky   will be full
     of them.   Soon, I will be
          back   on the kibbutz,
confessing.   I will drink
                         arak with men,   smoke
                         nargila with men. I
     will feel the night
                         change, air cooler,
          stars brighter.

Barcelona

Your hair is bright blonde to your
hips. Six months of desert sun. Six months of
nargila arak Hebrew Arabic. Here, you can
speak. You can read signs, order a glass of wine.
Vino, por favor. You can ask for directions, tell
men to fuck off. You're fatter than you want to be,
but aren't you always? Tonight, a woman wants
you. Dark haired, white polka dots on a black dress.
Takes your hand. Skin so soft you think you might
fall through it. Leads you through a crowd
of men to the street. Lights two cigarettes.
Your hair is sun, she says in English. You smile,
inhale. It's not the truth: this calm, cool
inhale. Your own hand wet and trembling.
You're too young and dumb and afraid
to look at her the way she looks at you.
Her name is Eva. She kisses your cheek,
you blush. You leave her in the street, feel her
eyes on your back. You don't turn around.

To Think That I Could Be a Mother

Streets with their dramatic peaks and valleys, fog that buries skyscrapers and the great gold bridge over choppy gray water. This is the city at night, and you're drunk. You've started at a bar and then a friend's house. You're in the street now, at an intersection with a bottle. You take the last swig and throw the bottle up in the air, its clear glass refracts the streetlights. A floating crystal, it kisses the telephone wires and shatters back down. Your friends are not impressed. They shake their heads at your destruction. You want to explain how the bottle left your hands, how sometimes bottles do. You want them to understand tonight when you try to steal the champagne from the Safeway on Market, you are and are not trying to prove something. You want them to understand when you run through the train tunnel, you do and do not have something to lose. And when you sleep in Dolores Park, your friend's jacket a shared blanket, three chihuahuas nipping you awake to a clear hungover morning, you want them to know you're not sure where the line is and when and how far you've crossed over it.

Grandmother Ethel

I did not know her. I did not know her car
with the antlers tied to the roof. I did not
know her after gin, how she held her
anger. I did not know the specific way
she parted her hair. Serious, tall. Pretty
but not very. I know she is said to have been
like me. Not in shape but in mood. Perpetual
shifting. Once she threw a glass against
a wall. Once I hurled a stone through
a glass table. Once the glass shattered,
we cleaned it up bare-handed: some bodies
want to be punished. We scream
at our lovers and our loves. Stan left her
and the country, ran a sailing company
in Honduras. Michael moved from me
to New York, fought for union rights, maybe
married the lover who wrote a book
about motorcycles. He left in the spring. A man
on her porch in March, suitcase packed, last
cigarette crushed to the wood with his heel. Both
of us pleading. Both of us drunk. Cannot look
ourselves in the eyes. Take the car out
for a drive. Buy and buy. Here is a shirt, love.
Here a book, lover. We buy bottles:
whiskey, gin. Scream at whoever remains.
She had seven children. Breast cancer
that spread to the brain.
In the end, she was wrapped
in the sheets of a hospital bed.
Her daughter, my mother, on a plane.

We Would Have Said

Remember the ways our bodies
swayed, drunk to Daft Punk?
Beside us, the man on acid
waved a spatula, hand trembling.
You pointed, laughed. Desert
night peeled open eyelids. A whole
fresh world, cool evening grass.
Dried sweat: our new layer of
skin. We ran through crowds
like children, hands joined
like lovers. This was years
ago. You're married now. A girl
and a boy of your own. No invite
to your wedding, just the quiet
distance between us. Once, we
would have said, it should have
been us. The way you watched me
brush my teeth one night in Berkeley.
Fog milky at the window, cold
damp tile, yellow light. Side by side
in the mirror. *Gentle*, you said.
I brushed and brushed
until my gums bled.

The Farm

Carob tree in the center, its curling pods. And strange lines like roots dangling from branches. Color in distinct swaths, earth tones. Tones of the land. Two structures on either side, one an animal enclosure, the other a barn. And between them, a path leading to a woman. I wonder about that woman. I wonder about myself, standing before the painting. In London, though I remember it being Paris. Hemingway's favorite painting. I read a story about him buying it, and imagine it strapped to the roof of a car. He kept it above his bed. I know the image I kept above mine. A photograph: an eagle hunter in Mongolia. The same clear blue sky. A block of blue. Negative space. In the painting, a moon. In the photograph, nothing. Just sky and the half-silhouette of a man with an eagle. Wings outstretched. A man painted the painting, a man took the photograph too. An Israeli man who touched me in my sleep, uninvited. And then I frame and hang his photograph above my bed. Just like I'm not supposed to love Hemingway. A man's man. The books too direct, too violent, too much for my womanness. And yet, I like the painting because of him. Hemingway's favorite. I like the photograph because of him: a warning. Memory of a man in the sheets. Memory of his touch. Memory of waking. Memory of what the fuck. Memory of standing in front of the painting. I don't notice the lizard in the foreground, the agave along the path. Hands where I don't want them. Memory of anger. Memory at a museum looking.

You Burn Me

after Sappho

Throat dry, four whiskeys deep,
I feel your hands on my shoulders,
holding me.

That familiar embrace. Lover. Intimacy
so violent. I am not supposed to desire
you. Morning now—the wing beside me tilts

against the golden light. Below,
the landscape is ravaged by heat. Water
once carved out its path here, and wind:
unrelenting scars across the earth.

I sip another whiskey, force it past
my lips. Morning: the flight attendant
glares at me. Her smile a line.
Soon I'll be on the ground again.

Memory of you gleaming under sweat,
under sunlight, under me.
I would leave you here in the air,

but I still feel you
in my throat, I feel you
in my throat,
burning.

New Year

Light on redwood trunks, stars full silver, glittering lake in a wet green valley. Music so loud it hurts. Acid, champagne: shivering in the night. Branches contort into faces. Jaw clenches. He cannot stand me anymore, he decides, one section of branches the face of my second-grade teacher. Bird-like and blonde with a small upturned nose—Mrs. Pitter. I read my first novel in her class: *Black Beauty.* The branches once faces now horses. I giggle. *Really*, he says, *I think I hate you.* We're in the grass, our asses wet, our hands wet. Wet grass smell. Like country, like fresh morning. Like horses. He looks me over: my legs, my breasts, my neck, my face. He shakes his head. *Sorry*, he says. He says, *Sorry*, and stands. I flatten my back to the grass: kaleidoscopic stars. His voice at a distance. Later, he will drive me in silence to his house, line the bed center with pillows: *I don't want to touch you*, he will explain. This man. My lover. Hand in the cold wet grass.

Paros

Hillside of tiny flames,
stretch of orange crumbled
cliffs, a fig tree—roots breaking
through cobblestones, trunk carved
with letters. Fishermen leave
their nets in piles along the waterfront.
Blue domed, white walled churches,
crooked streets, a farmer's market with
too many onions. The church of a hundred
doors does not have a hundred doors. It is not
blue or white, but brown gone gold
in the last evening light. On the clothesline
beside a restaurant is the body
of an octopus. Around the corner is
my flat. Blue shutters, white
paint. A full rooftop deck. I buy
ouzo in liters and wear sandals
into the sea. The sand is home
to urchins: purple balls of spines.

Some women are quiet about
illness. Mine is not the quiet kind.
Mine keeps me up at night. Takes me
to the sea, naked. Leads me
to bars alone. Drinks glass after glass
of ouzo. Dances and climbs
walls, breaks boots on tree trunks.
Limps home again. Wakes to a man
in bed, hands up my shirt. Mine is
the kind of illness that orders
the octopus on credit card. Uses
the payphone by the sea to call
home. Forgets lovers, friends. Smokes
the cigarettes in the gold foil
boxes. Thinks maybe I will stay
among statues: fine-grained, pure-white,
translucent, buried beneath
the Aegean, unyielding, flawless.

Against Her

after Sappho

four steps to the phonebooth
you could have her in your

arms just her body breaking
under touch the scarf at her neck

a noose you have seen her before
the one with violets in her lap

here is the anchor of her
scalp the hard plastic phone

cradle here is your whole
self against her whole self

the one with violets in her lap
writhing fighting here is your

sloppy drunk mouth and the
edge of her jaw clamped tight

against you your lips moving
across her lips against her cheek

you will teach her skin purple
flesh balled up in your fists

the one with violets in her lap
fuck the violets she will learn

to hate pretty things can't you
see she doesn't want you doesn't

know you and she is just a woman
you should know all women learn

the value of stones stolen fragments
of sea folded into palms

dead weight in our pockets.

How to Write a Poem Without *Woman* or *Body*

Use the words *girl* or *female*. Write about fingertips
and elbows. But don't forget this cage of muscle and
bone, the familiar and unfamiliar feel of eyes on legs,
eyes on breasts, eyes on ass. The ways in which you
can never relinquish your sex. If you were a man
you would smile with your head down to the pavement.
Catch every door for every person wanting to pass through.
Remember that your body (there it is) moves over
sidewalks with ease. But you are not a man, you are
a woman (and there she is). You did not design yourself
this way. Breasts and hips. You wish it were otherwise.
That your body (and again) was a flat straight line.
A neutral grace to your step. (A fantasy.) You don't mean
to write poems about bodies (or women), you just
mean to write poetry. You can write about trees—
the cypress on the cliffs (was it Santa Cruz?), their jagged
wind-bent branches. Cottonwoods (in so many arroyos)
in New Mexico or the ones that lean over that park path
in Salt Lake. Or maybe return to the Sonoran Desert
(that you love so dearly). Cholla piling up to the sun,
prickly pear scattered across dirt. Stop collapsing in
(on yourself), finding ways to make metaphors about
kneecaps, about skin. What is it like to watch the world (melt)?
The body (of a woman) walking. Kicking through piles
of yellow gingko leaves in Indiana. Waiting for winter. (Waiting.)

III

Coalesce

And the dew on the grass after a night full up of air from the Pacific,
it's there glittering like translucent pearls, like tiny bodies clinging.

And the feeling of teeth against knuckle, two fingers
probing the back of your throat: you should stop, you should stop.

And the redwood trees outside the house,
the stick-straight tall of them. Soft bark, feathered leaves.

And you in the bathroom, staring down the mirror, pull at the flesh
of the hips, suck in the stomach, raise the jaw away from the neck.

And outside is spring again. Daffodils freed from their winter slumber,
apple trees and plum trees and apricot alive with blossom.

And you are afraid he might hear you so you run the sink,
the shower as though California had water enough forever.

And in the backyard, spilling over the fence line in the summertime,
are the blackberries, the berries you love best, plump and dense and sweet.

And the fruit taking over blossom like a woman undressing
in moonlight. Moon in the window and the room and you with your body

afraid of what it could hold if you let it.

How is this Supposed to End

Beneath the table, arms crossed
over my belly: this food isn't for me.

No food is.
I am not eating. Not salmon or rice or broccoli.
I drink wine. Deep red stains
on my lips, my teeth.

They do not talk to me: my mother,
her best friend and the husband.

Then, suddenly, they do. Or: he does.
The husband. The man.
He's drunk on beer and sunlight. His face
irredeemably red.

What if you slept in my bed?

We women study our plates, mine full, theirs empty.
I hold my belly tighter: a torniquet.

He is like an uncle to me. As a child,
I sat on his lap. His wife changes the subject:

Are you going to eat that?

I shake my head.
But he, the husband, the man, my uncle,
persists. To my mother, he winks,

Tonight, we can trade places.

Earlier, he was speaking of my beauty. My hair,
my little female figure.

Before that, he was my uncle, folding me into
an embrace. Telling me how grown up I have become.
Now, he is drunk and I want   to be anything other than
woman.

It is smallness I desire. To become less
than I am. To turn sideways
and vanish. Press my belly to my spine.

I look at my full plate and then up at my uncle: his red drunk face,
eyes with a certain ugly shimmer.
How is this supposed to end?

My mother says nothing.
But later, she locks the door to our room
and when she thinks I am sleeping,   she slips

out of bed and checks it. Twisting
the brushed nickel one way
and then the other,
a small metal sound in the night.

I Can't Get Off the Floor

Day bright, sun-riddled. Sky insistent blue. I can't get off the floor. I can see the window: sky, brightness. Sun hits skin, warms back, arms, legs. Naked on the floor and can't get up. Yesterday, in group, a mother spoke of her daughter. A mother should not be in group. Only daughters. To think that I could be a mother. No. I am a daughter and cannot get off the floor. Knocking at the door now. My mother. Let her knock and knock. She jiggles the doorknob: locked. Sighs and says coffee, breakfast. She says, come downstairs. Says she knows I'm awake. Remember a time at the ocean with my mother. Holding her hand. The waves crashed at our shins, one after another, buried our feet in velvet sand. And then a wave we couldn't predict. Knocked us down, broke us apart. Mother screaming. I could not get up. The sea had me, pulling, dragging me out and down. And then my mother above: forcing me to my feet, a rescue. And now, my mother at the door, begging. Come downstairs. Mother. I can't get off the floor.

Windows Open to the Night

Sometimes I forget myself, stray
into a bar alone. Whiskey neat please.
And no, I don't want to talk to you. No,
I am not married. See here? No glittering
metal band around my finger. Just this glass
of liquid gold in my fist. And yes, I am afraid
all the time. Coyote Joe's at two am, and I know
he didn't plan to follow me. I hit the pavement

running—I always wear boots I can run in, I say
to whoever will listen. Never know when I have
to. The moon in its silver swagger there
at the horizon, casting everything death shade.
I've never shot a gun. Never want to. I don't want
that cold heavy metal in my hand, that sound
of ruin in my ears. I just want what I can't have:
a bar, a whiskey, my moonlit walk home alone.

One story I remember: a man, a woman
fighting. The man leaves, walks the neighborhood
at night because he can. The woman paces
the backyard, counting steps between chicken coop,
mesquite tree, circling the small cholla. The story
ends with the man crying: he realizes she is trapped
in the yard and he is free. The two make love,
windows open to the night.

In the real story, the man doesn't realize shit.
The fight lasts until morning. Until she takes
enough pills to fall asleep. And in the daylight,
he says, I'm hitting the restart button. That is his
apology. Hitting. And I stay with him for two more
years. In the end, it isn't the man who follows me
home from the bar, it is the man who,
in the shower, combs out my hair.

Teacup Rose

Yesterday by the teacup roses, I lost sight of myself. I stared down at my arms—streaked with blood from deadheading the front yard. I didn't recognize my limbs. Not my legs, not my elbows or biceps or wrist bones. It seemed so easy, for a moment, to be something else. A man perhaps. In leather gloves and spandex, out in front of my house on a Monday. The petals of the large pink rose fell to the ground, a littering of beauty. Their satin skin strewn across the succulents. My partner thinks to rake them up, to dispose of them, but I refuse. Too much like romance: a scatter of petals on a bed. My partner doesn't like roses. Too much the flower of boomers, he says. He likes the teacup rose best though, if he had to choose. So unlike the rest. Small buds, scentless, low to the ground. There by the roses he doesn't hate, I wondered if he would prefer me someone else. A dancer. A journalist. A woman with a career and an exercise routine. I studied my legs: the thighs, the kneecaps, the shin bones. I slipped into that other reality: man. Then I stared at the flawless tiny red blossoms, unlocked the shears and began.

Threshold

He pushed her outside // inside maybe.
he may have pushed her / inside. / a threshold,
and she crossed it: cold kitchen tile // snow drift porch.
Splintered wood // sandstone. Indiana // Arizona.

This woman: five stories up / two rooftops
air between. This is San Francisco! Wind / fog,
the paint bucket she'll piss in / later. She's
back // forth // drunk // unreasonable.

Indiana, on her knees // in his kitchen
where last week, he poured wine / reasonable.
Lucky he isn't much / a monster. What is a wrist
recolored? Skin stain // wine // bruise

The door is the threshold / the skin
is. If she didn't have it / he wouldn't
bruise it. But, Indiana in winter:
nothing keeps / its color.

He pushes her outside // Arizona // in a hallway.
Lucky, she isn't much / a woman. Sideways just
a sliver on a mattress/ it's his bed isn't it? She
is the threshold, then the air // the roof // the skin.

If she wasn't // didn't // he wouldn't.

Anatomy Lesson

after Ada Limón

You chop an onion across
from me, its edge in the air.
The strained, the quiet
muffled snowfall outside. For hours,
nothing but white beyond the window.
Your thoughts on anatomy,
the ways a body can break.
My study: the five noble grapes.
Sweetness, acidity, tannin, alcohol, body.
As a child, I was excited about daffodils,
stems unfurling from the earth,
soft white heads opening.
Paperwhites with their duplicitous
pale clusters. Large cupped ice follies
with their yellow centers. I beheaded
them all, filled a tray of water,
presented it to my mother. She shrieked,
I wept. The odor of onion drifting.
You ignore me and chop another:
isn't that enough? The luminous remains.
Chardonnay, Riesling, Sauvignon Blanc.
Heart, lungs, stomach, liver.
Later, you will practice on my body:
here the kidneys, there an artery.
Outside, the snow is picking up.
By morning, the driveway will be
thick with it. Night: this cold white
reckoning. And who doesn't know
the myth? Narcissus in love with his reflection,
two onions, on a cutting board, shattered.

She Climbs In

Sun burning through snow, releasing
        tulips, daffodils, freeing lawns
        from their winter white. Glass of bourbon,
no, daiquiri. Tropical, exotic. Impossible.

Pretend I do not give a shit about words.
        I'm a doctor. I care about organs and blood.
        I have money to spend on vacations. I stay
at the resort because I want serenity and

thousand thread-count sheets.
        I want breakfast in bed, and a newspaper
        on my doorstep. Forget about boys, about doctors.
About him. Never meet him at all.

I'm in a bathtub near an ocean.
        My lover in the kitchen, cooking something
        decadent. She comes into the bathroom
where I have my whole face submerged.

Carries a piña colada, fresh coconut, fresh pineapple.
        Caresses me to the surface of the water,
        smooths the hair from my forehead.
She climbs in, clothes on. The wet fabric clinging.

Photograph: Tucson Mountains

I like this one for my jawline. The bone there making me look thinner than I am. All angle and light. Once, a friend told me he only liked women with visible collarbones. Body so thin you could see the lines of the ribcage. In the photograph, the light is soft—dusk. Saguaros in shadow, rock a muted red. The problem is he's got his mouth on mine: a kiss. Man I met in the desert. Engineering man. Running man. He is maybe a good man, but we are not good for each other. You wouldn't know from the photograph. The way his face opens to mine. The gentle light. Eyes closed. Sketch of a roadrunner on my neck. I haven't had to run for years now. Forgetting the hollow sound of shoes against pavement. The desire to flee. Desire. We won't misunderstand each other in the end: the dusty landscape with its splash of green palo verde. We can only move in directions apart. In the desert, we're kissing. Eyes closed on camera but in a moment they'll be open again.

You have to run open mouthed

after "Frida Kahlo to Marty McConnell"

to winter. Your body is Indiana
strung between better states.
You found a man who thought
everything worthy was broken,
wanted to fix roofs and engines
and you, foolish girl. Now you must
dismantle his story. Run to the
desert and bury your heels in
the waterless earth. Let your nights
be long and whiskey-weathered. Let
men touch you who don't deserve
hands and then tell them that.
Crush chiles in your kitchen,
cook them into sauce into
your lips. Wear lace on the outside.
Let your hair grow long. Tattoo
your neck, your chest, your thighs.
Stupid girls are always trying
to scrub their skin clear.

And you are not stupid. You are full
of knots, ringed with memory.
You have legs as resilient as cacti
and you can plant them anywhere.

IV

Sonoran Desert

At night, a dreamscape of shapes,

spikes gone soft in starlight.

trail between their water-logged

forms luminous. Proud saguaro sentinels:

stand up straight, stand up straight.

I haven't come to the desert for its beauty,

but for its scarcity. The way water pools

and streams out across great swaths of land.

I want to know what it's like to live without

something. Not something, but someone.

Stars spilled like salt

across the table of sky. The fresh clean

creosote smell. Soft glowing

teddy bear cholla, wraith-like
ocotillo limbs,

indistinct clumps of brittle bush. Coyotes in the

distance. Moonrise over mountains, sucking up

stars, turning the world silver. I think
about

how just yesterday I wanted to sleep

forever. This is what

my therapist calls death.

But I wonder. We say forever when we mean

for as long as we can stand. Sometimes,

that isn't long at all. Bats slip like shadows

through the air. I should turn around now,

but before me is a forest of silhouettes,

a study in mortality, a great open desert full

and awake and belonging to no one.

Fire

Cracked heartwood litters my driveway, outside
in a tank top in December. Saguaro-studded.
Cholla and so many spines. This isn't my home,
won't ever be. Home is where the fires are. Paradise
and Coffey Park. Alarms at two a.m. and the smell
like campfire like smoke. Like choosing between
a portrait of a grandmother I never knew and the owl
painting of my childhood. Like the way, bumper
to bumper, we held each other not with affection
but with fire. In the desert, I carry the cottonwood
remains from driveway to hearth. Strike a match,
heat on my chest. When I tell you, I am not
home, it doesn't mean I want to be. Newspaper
gives me all I need to know about waiting. Charred
body on a lawn gripping a garden hose. A mother
and son on a road, running. One lone chimney
like a punchline to some joke. When I tell you
the evacuation I experienced was precaution and
order. When I admit that I want to feel the heat
until it's upon me or maybe I feel it inside me.
Three cigarettes into the skin near my knuckles.
Do you know how it scorched? How it scarred?
To be in some other state, some other crisis.
Away from that clogged night sky.
Do you know what it means to start over?
So much left behind. So much I can't return to,
don't want to. On that early morning in the line
of cars, I wondered what it would be like to lose,
to grieve all the things of my life. A small ugly
thrill. I didn't have to leave. Didn't have to move
to the desert where the earth takes water like my skin
took those embers. Where outside is the trunk
of a cottonwood, an axe. Stoke the fire, they say,
because without me, it could die. Its container
the only thing that might survive it. I don't know
which way is north without a star, which way is west
without an ocean. It means I don't know where
to run to. Maybe none of us do.

Nephew

For Carlin Lieu Bell

My brother's son, my   nephew.
His stubby soft toes, the   open-mouthed
smile, reaching for   his mother's arms.
An affection I can't explain,   and a sadness.
The next generation: shared litany of what is   inherited.

Grandfather Stan—   his tendency to leave and leave
behind, his World War II   PTSD
Or the Jews   we lost
on my father's side.   All the alcoholism
from my mother's. My mental illness.   And what about

the Field temper? The way it   simmers and spills
over—collateral damage.   I can't look
at him without thinking   about water, about fire.
So much to lose. I wonder   will there be books
still? And who will be allowed   to author them?

I hold him with one arm, awkward.   My sister-in-law says
he loves me. And I have   no children of my own.
Because they   cry and cry and
I don't know how to help them.   What to say:
I'm sorry.   I'm so sorry

we aren't better   than we are.
Human, after all.   As though,
the city where he   lives will not be affected
by rising oceans,   by earthquakes,
by the hollowing out   of the Hetch Hetchy.

As though   he himself—
Chinese on his mother's side—   will not be altered
by the way this country sees him.   Not white enough. I hold
him,   feel his weight drag at
my muscles.   I am afraid

I will drop him. I hold tighter, and   see my brother
smile, watching his sister   hold his son.

Looking at Your Body

I.
Ache. A hollowing out. Remember
the time with the woman who
ordered marrow from the menu.
Two bones balanced on a plate. How
you spooned and sucked at the insides.
Fat and blood. The bone at your lips.

II.
Unworry your fingers from their
knot. Skin and knuckle.
Clamped together. Pressure.
You could be so much
more if you wanted.

III.
Fever dream. Man on a rooftop hurling
himself through air to another rooftop.
Your indecision at the edge. All that space.
Pavement below. The woman who
pulled you back, saying, *Don't be
stupid. Don't.* Day you realized
something about women: trust.

IV.
Deceit and desire and desire and
desire. The lover in your quivering
arms, in the frozen Midwest winter.
Trees outside skeletons. Inside
the room is ice and the way the
two of you fit and do
not fit together.

V.
Undo the expectations of
your appendages. Feet attached by
a kind of hinge. Tendon and bones
settled into each other. Toe pointed,
ankle flexed. Line from shin to toe:
an exclamation mark.

VI.
Remember the tragic falling of
that bird's nest. Sparrows or finches.
Something small and unmemorable.
Still, you saw the dog and
screamed. He swallowed the
barely-feathered babies whole,
smacking his lips.

VII.
Breathe. Difficult at altitude. That
thinness, the tilted mountains—jagged,
snow-capped. Slick wet rocks, landscape
studded with wildflowers. You couldn't
find your way home if you tried.

VIII.
Sleep with the stranger at the bar, the
stranger at the restaurant, the stranger
with the wife, with the husband.
You're not that kind of woman.

IX.
Sometimes it's better to pretend:
your niece and your nephew with
the pillow fort. One of them insists,
This is mine. The other insists, *This is mine.*

X.
Behind the wheel, ninety on the 101.
Ocean crashing to one side. You could
be anywhere, but you're here.
In California with your history and
your lover and a car full of you
and your will to escape.

Wolf Painting

I'm in the bathtub again. Always in the bathtub these days. I sit in the bathtub and then on the couch and then back in the bathtub. Painted above me is a trio of wolves by a river the color of the Aegean. A turquoise I'd like to sink into. To wrap my body inside of. To eat. It's a color I have been in—over a decade ago. I skinny-dipped in the Aegean at night when it was the color of tar. The turquoise I saw when I ran along the coast in the day. I wanted to fling myself into it. An embrace of a landing. An embrace. I sit in the bathtub and drink and stare down at my body. Below the surface is the fear of my body alone and older and so riddled with imperfection. I wonder who will want this body when he doesn't? The wolves above me are a family. An adult and two pups. One pup sniffs the dirt, the other pup howls, and the adult wolf drinks from the river, sending out a circle of ripples. I imagine her female. Because of course I do. Once, in Athens, I was at a bar with only white paint, white furniture, white everything. I was with three men, American, my colleagues. One man couldn't handle his liquor, never could. He climbed the bar and began dancing. Or maybe he tried to climb the bar, and we restrained him. Either way, I remember the glow of the place: all that white. Like being inside of paper. A blankness. The wolves: their presence looming over me. I've never seen one in the wild. I've heard them though, howling

Oysters

In the Midwest, I eat oysters. Slick, briny
flesh. Texture of shell—wavy edges.
Rough exterior, smooth wet inside. Bed
of rock salt. Mignonette in a metal dish
and horseradish. I am not near
an ocean. West coast or east coast or
a combination of the two. Like deciding
where to go next. This way, that way,
a combination of the two. Living outside of my
surroundings, of my means: oysters in the Midwest.
I prefer west, but I'm thirty-six now, and I wonder
about the Atlantic. States piled against coastline.
Where to make a home, a place for
my red couches, my cat, my plants. Order
a martini—gin, dirty. Watch the bartender
strain out ice crystals. I like ice crystals.
I like the three salty olives on a toothpick.
The bottles behind the bar, trapping chandelier
light. And the suited bartender who
says *Miss* instead of *Ma'am*. Who says to me
with his eyes, *you don't belong here, but*
I'm willing to pretend. For oysters,
for gin. Atlantic, Pacific. Back in my current home,
the life I live isn't the life I want to. The man there,
the credit card debt. Mountains and parks.
Winter in the high desert. My backyard with
the irises I will not see bloom again. The lilac
I will never smell. Here I sip gin, stare at the bottles,
pretend I don't have to make any decision beyond
east or west. I suck down one after another,
the sea on my tongue.

Last Week

Wednesday
Summer: air too hot, too dry. He reports that the squash blossoms form and fall without fruit. I haven't been outside in days. Not because of the weather. Can't seem to leave the couch. First coffee then beer then whiskey. There isn't enough water anyway.

Thursday
Difficult to see the way the days could stretch and take shape. Individuate. Today's gray or maybe yesterday. Or tomorrow. However the day works, there's thunder and lightning in the night: breaking over us. The house—our house—shudders. He sleeps on beside me. I stare at the ceiling, counting the cracks.

Friday
And another. He'll be leaving soon, his life packed into his car, my life left here alone in our house. He hardly visits the garden anymore. Snipping suckers from tomato elbows. Staking peppers and sunflowers. Can't look at the hand-built trellis, the boxes with the bench.

Saturday
He is something manic. Roots around the tomatoes and brings to the couch a green zebra, a golden sunrise. Slices and salts and arranges them in an arc of color. I slide them off the plate and chase them down with wine. Decadent if the wine were something special. *I plan on drinking my way through this,* I tell anyone who will listen.

Sunday
Walk. Outside. Disappointed by the muted green, the drooping sunflowers by the sidewalk. I never understood his love of order, of logic. Green stalks equally spaced: a neat and tidy row. I love the jungle of them—squirrel scattered seeds. Sky an unsettling clean slate. I haven't been sober in weeks.

Monday
Sad sex, he calls it. And it is. The aching. The familiar unfamiliar. The leaving. Pillow talk is where he'll go next. New Mexico, Arizona, North Carolina. He shrugs and pulls me to his chest. The heat, the skin.

Tuesday
He cries like he sneezes. Loud. It makes me blush. I hold him to me. Outside the garden is still the garden, but inside the house which is our house is my house now. Of me. He's on the porch. We smoke a cigarette. And another.

Four Walls Become a Woman

Who shall measure the heat and violences of the poet's heart
when caught and tangled in a woman's body? —Virginia Woolf

I can measure it here, where the morning light spills
across the page, and my legs are thrown into shadow.
Or there, where outside the window redwood trees
tower over wall, over roof, softening the rising sun.

I found myself in a book again, not me but my body.
This heavy thing they call woman. Another man writing
my inner monologue. Another man thinking about pregnancy,
motherhood. But what of the myriad ways I desire?

The urgency to fill a page with words. Sex, too, but sometimes
I'd rather just be alone in a forest. I imagine a cabin.
Jumble of tree trunks needing to be turned to firewood. Shirtless
as any man, with my axe, cracking open the orange centers.

Men write me as if they understand walls. Four walls:
a room for this woman's body. If I'm being an optimist:
my cabin. But most likely a track home in suburbia.
Ripe and full with another child. Wife. Mother.

Or perhaps a mistress, a temptress: riddled with desire
for him. The manic pixie dream of his dream. I'd be thin
as a waif in a fairytale. I'd smoke cigarettes, drink vodka.
I'd sleep on silk sheets and steal thongs from department stores.

We'd stay in hotels, order bottles of champagne. I'd tell him
I've done this for him, for his desire. I'd lie. Things I've done
for men: lie. On my back. On my belly. I am between his walls,
his hotel's sheets, our bodies not our bodies, together.

Between my walls, in my room, there is no body. Woman or otherwise. My
walls are my own. My words are of water, my windows, light.

Heart

He says, *What's wrong?* He's always
noticing. This new man: my lover,
my partner. I tell him, *my heart.*
He rests his head on my bare chest,
his ear to my skin. *Abnormal,*
he murmurs. My heart picks up
its pace. I am always wanting
him. Other nights, when my heart
is normal, he bites into my neck,
my chest, my sides. His teeth, not
gentle, but something I can point
to, sometimes a small light bruise.

Sometimes it is my mother's heart
that drives me to panic. Her chest
butterflied open, organs hooked
to machines, frail bones supported
by a plate. I imagine a dinner plate,
one from my childhood: navy
with white flowers. Her heart is
repaired now, valve replaced with
bovine flesh that can only last
so long. Her life on a clock, ticking.

In bed, with my lover: he says
hospital. There, I'd really panic, under
the florescence, let my eyes go dark
with light. I'd want him there beside
me, his hand on my hand. I'd want
to call my mother. Failed
muscle. Lover by my side. My heart
at home, thrumming under
the weight of his skull, his hand on
my ribs, his cheek on my breast. I
think about how much I want
his skin on my skin, how much
I want to stay in this body
a little longer still.

O'Keeffe Country

And here it is. Or there. Or maybe
it's all of this state with its hot red
rock and bright green cottonwoods.
Skies so big they could swallow
you. And they do. All that blue.
The puffed up clouds, the low close
air. The soft dirt underfoot, under
fingernail. Always putting myself
into what doesn't concern me.
Clay cups that quick-dry and cannot
hold liquid. What is the use
of the thing? The way it looks
shaped by my own hands. On a
desk or counter. Some memory
of O'Keeffe. Iris. Hollyhock.
Cala lily. Landscape so vague
it's uninhabitable. Just lines and
color. So much that doesn't belong
to me. Just passing through. Looking
for whatever I can take. A white bone
in a forest of orange trees. Ponderosas.
Jaw of something great and full
of life. Now paled by sun and heat
and weather. White as a cloud. White
as porcelain. White as bone. I look
to the sky again. Clear, blue. Now
empty. Just expanse. Just color. Just
the way we can continue when we
forget. When bones are just bones
and maybe this is just country.
The way the whole place expands
beyond every horizon. This spit of
land, this muddy river, that cliff,
that crag. O'Keeffe writes,
"I picked them up and took them
home too." She means bones.
She means rocks. She means flowers.
Sky. Dirt. Tree. The whole country
she painted. What it means
to paint something. To write.

All that taking. All that blue.

ACKNOWLEDGMENTS:

This book would not exist without the teachers of my life who helped me to be a student, a person, and ultimately a writer: Gary Young, Uri Gordon, Melanie Bishop, Sheila Sanderson, K.L. Cook, Zoe Hammer, George Crane, Larry Felson, Allison Lynn. And of course, I have to thank all the incredible faculty at New Mexico State University for making me the writer that I am today, especially: Coach Rus Bradburd, Connie Voisine, the late Lee K. Abbott, Evan Lavender-Smith, Richard Greenfield, the late Mark Medoff, Carmen Giménez, and Lily Hoàng. Finally, thanks to Lindsey Drager for the unending support and to Jackie Osherow for encouraging me to keep writing poems and for the generous and loving feedback.

A special thanks to Pam Houston for her mentorship and words: I'm not sure I'd still be standing if it weren't for Pam. And thanks to Writing by Writers for the incredible opportunities I've had to build community and share and write.

Thanks to the Taft-Nicholson Center for being the perfect place for poetry. And thanks to all the folks who fund and organize the Steffensen Cannon Fellowship. I could not have written this book without the generous support I've received.

Thank you to the folks at Finishing Line who believed in this book; especially thanks to Leah Huete de Maines, Mimi David, and Christen Kincaid.

Thank you to Sarah Williams for her brilliant cover art. I am forever indebted to you for your vision for this book and for your incredible talent as a painter.

To my writing community here in Salt Lake City. This book is especially possible because of Jasmine Khaliq's brilliant editorial advice and Jessica Tanck's belief in its potential. Thanks also and always to Jamie Smith, Matty Layne Glasgow, Vitasta Singh, Meagan Arthur, Audrey Bauman, Jake Yordy, Chengru He, Aristotle Johns, Garrett Biggs, Daniel Uncapher, and Jesse Kohn.

And to my greater writing community: Zeeda Anderson, who wrote poetry with me as a teenager; Evan Belknap, my college writing buddy; my NMSU crew—Brady Richards, Patrick Stockwell, Emily Alex, Josh Randall, Emily Cook, Brooke Sahni, Barry Pearce, and Marzie Ghasempour; my Writing by Writers loves—Chaya Ungar, Caro Kay, Shirley Chan, and Mark Gross. Thanks also to Hannah Wederquist-Keller: we shall eat all the hearts together. And to my new poetry-writing bestie, Jess Eagle. Thank you all: you are all so invaluable to my writing and my life.

Every book I write will forever be indebted to Tara Westmor and Diana Clarke. Tara: thank you for your love and care and drive to write and for digging me out of the pit when I needed it most. Clarke: thank you for all the writing retreats, for your careful and loyal reading of my words, and for always knowing when to tough-love me when I need it. I would like to live on a commune with both of you please.

To Ilan Cohen and Tori and Sam and Luca: thank you for being my chosen family.

To Lauren Wallace, and to Morgan, Theo, and Lee: you are my SLC family, and now you will never be rid of me. Thank you.

To Kim and John and Dylan: I love you very much. Thank you for being such a big part of my life and for all the love and support.

To the rest of my family. My wonderful parents: you have made my writing career possible in so many ways and I cannot thank you enough. To my brother, Joe, and my sister-in-law Char, to my Aunt Pam and my Uncle Bill, to my cousin, Avrey, and to Meghan, and to Reese and Hana. And to Susan and MeeMaw and Jack and Johnny. To the Boyds and to Ted and Martina and Henry. Y'all make my family complete.

And finally to the next generation of my family: I am so proud to be your aunt. I love you very much: Carlin, Evrett, Harlan, Judah, and Eli.

Allison Field Bell is a multi-genre writer from Northern California. She holds a PhD in Creative Writing and English Literature from the University of Utah and an MFA in Creative Writing from New Mexico State University. Allison is a Fiction Editor for *Waxwing* and the Social Media Editor & Assistant Prose Poetry Editor for *Pithead Chapel*. Her debut short story collection, *Bodies of Other Women*, is the 2025 Winner of the Red Hen Press Women's Prose Prize, judged by Alyssa Graybeal. The book is forthcoming in 2028. She is also the author of two chapbooks out in the world now—*Edge of the Sea* (creative nonfiction, CutBank Books) and *Without Woman or Body* (poetry, Finishing Line Press)—and the flash fiction chapbook, *Stitch*, forthcoming 2026 with Chestnut Review Books. Find her at allisonfieldbell.com

www.ingramcontent.com/pod-product-compliance
Lightning Source LLC
LaVergne TN
LVHW090536110826
845146LV00003B/1135

* 9 7 9 8 8 9 9 9 0 3 9 6 0 *